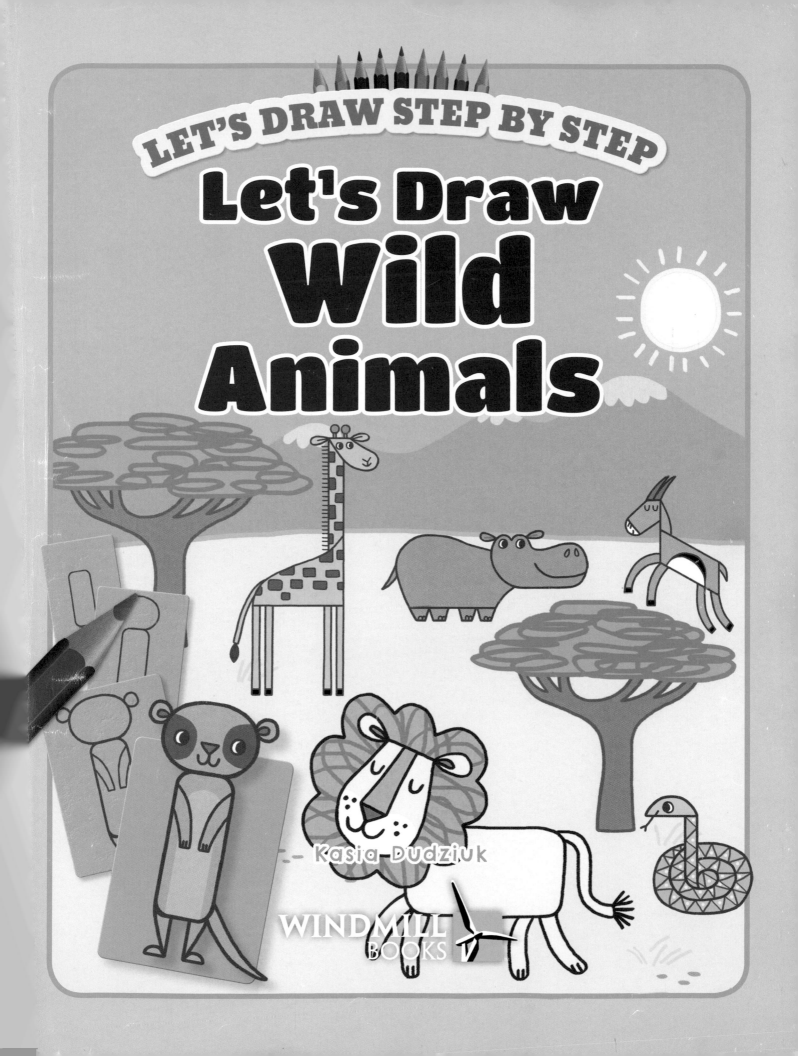

Published in 2017 by **Windmill Books**,
an Imprint of Rosen Publishing
29 East 21st Street, New York, NY 10010

Copyright © 2017 Arcturus Holdings Limited

Illustrations: Kasia Dudziuk
Text: JMS Books
Designer: Chris Bell
Editors: Joe Harris and Anna Brett

Cataloging-in-Publication Data
Names: Dudziuk, Kasia.
Title: Let's draw wild animals / Kasia Dudziuk.
Description: New York : Windmill Books, 2017. | Series: Let's draw step by step | Includes index.
Identifiers: ISBN 9781499481884 (pbk.) | ISBN 9781499481891 (library bound) | ISBN 9781508192930 (6 pack)
Subjects: LCSH: Animals in art--Juvenile literature. | Wildlife art--Juvenile literature. |
    Drawing--Technique--Juvenile literature.
Classification: LCC NC780.D83 2017 | DDC 743.6--dc23

Manufactured in the United States of America
CPSIA Compliance Information: Batch #BW17PK: For Further Information contact Rosen Publishing, New York, New York at 1-800-237-9932

Contents

Let's draw a zebra! 4

Draw a rhinoceros. 5

How about a crocodile? 6

Draw a hairy gorilla. 7

Let's draw an elephant. 8

Draw a tall giraffe. 9

What about a lion? 10

Try an elegant gazelle. 12

What about a hippo? 13

Let's draw a cheetah! 14

How about a meerkat? 15

Can you draw a shark? 16

Let's try an octopus. 17

Try drawing a dolphin. 18

Draw a great big whale! 19

Learn to draw a starfish. 20

Try a wise old owl. 21

Draw a caterpillar. 22

Now try a butterfly. 23

Let's draw a buzzy bee. 24

Now try a ladybug. 25

How about a reindeer? 26

Let's try a Pterodactyl. 27

Draw a Triceratops. 28

Then try a Diplodocus. 29

Glossary 30

Further reading 31

Websites 31

Index 32

Let's draw a zebra!

1 Here are his body and neck.

2 Now add his head and nose.

3 Don't forget his ears, legs and long tail!

4 Give him some lovely black stripes.

Draw a rhinoceros.

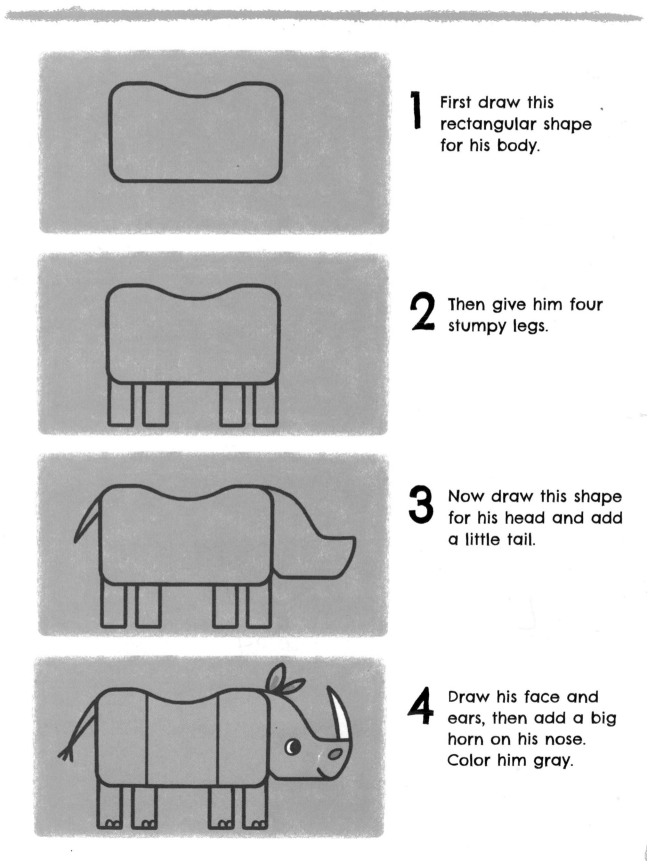

1 First draw this rectangular shape for his body.

2 Then give him four stumpy legs.

3 Now draw this shape for his head and add a little tail.

4 Draw his face and ears, then add a big horn on his nose. Color him gray.

How about a crocodile?

1 Start with a long box for his body.

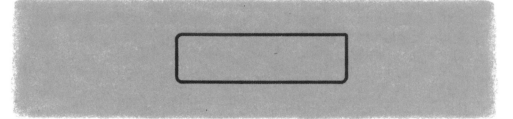

2 Add the shapes for his head and tail.

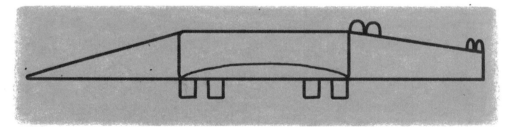

3 Don't forget his small legs, eyes and nostrils.

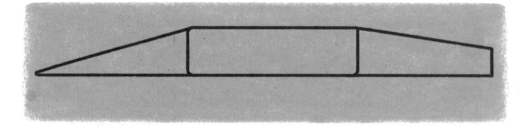

4 Add his teeth and the spines on his back. Color him green.

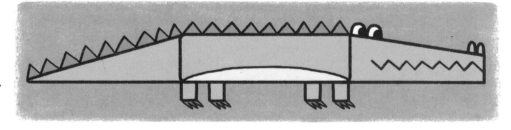

This is how to show him swimming in the water.

Draw a hairy gorilla.

1 Draw the shape of the gorilla's face.

2 Then add his two long arms.

3 Now draw his body. He is leaning forwards.

4 Draw his face and feet, and color him in.

Let's draw an elephant.

1 Here's his body.

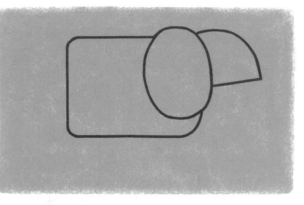

2 Give him a head and a big ear.

3 Add his curly trunk, thick legs and tail.

4 Color him gray. He looks very happy, doesn't he?

Can you draw a line of elephants?

There's a baby at the back!

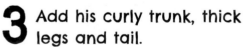

Draw a tall giraffe.

1 First draw this shape for his body.

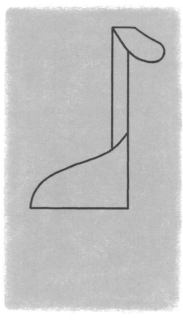

2 Add his head and long neck.

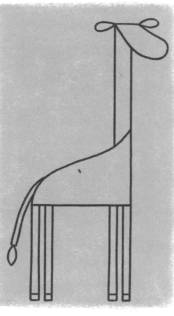

3 He has long legs, little ears and a tail as well!

4 Give him a face and two horns on top of his head.

9

What about a lion?

1 Draw his head and ears, surrounded by a mane.

2 Add his body.

3 He needs legs and a long tail!

4 Draw his face and color him in.

Here are some other big cats...

A lioness does not have a mane.

A leopard has a long curly tail.

His head is rounder than a lion's.

He is covered in spots.

He has a big chin.

A tiger has stripes.

Try an elegant gazelle.

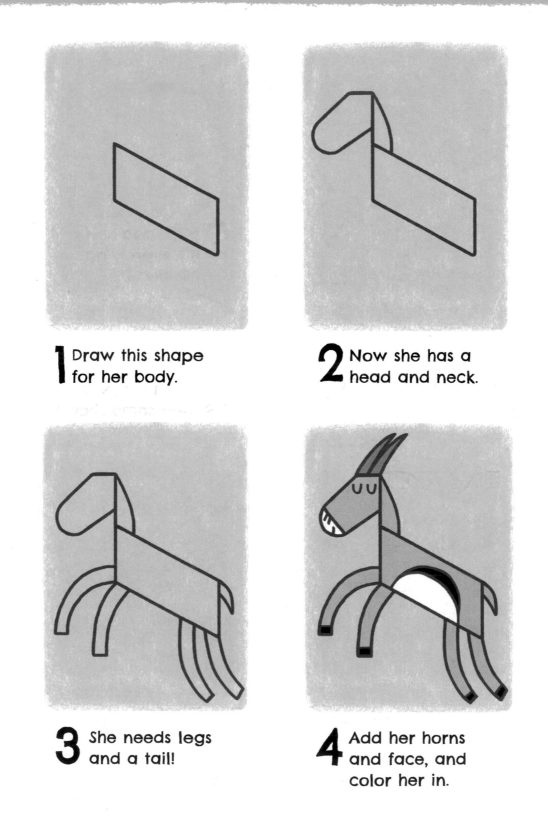

1 Draw this shape for her body.

2 Now she has a head and neck.

3 She needs legs and a tail!

4 Add her horns and face, and color her in.

What about a hippo?

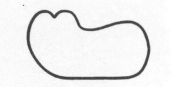

1 First draw the hippo's head. It's very big, isn't it?

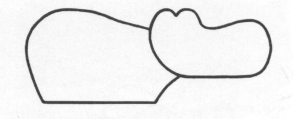

2 Now add his body. It's even bigger than his head.

3 Don't forget a little tail and some short legs.

4 Add his face and ears, and color him in. He looks very happy!

Try drawing him with his mouth open like this!

Let's draw a cheetah!

1 Start with a round head and ears.

2 Next draw a triangular shape for her body.

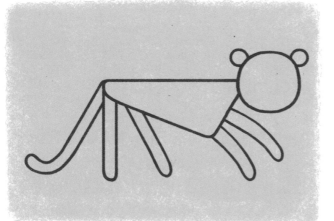 

3 She needs a tail and long legs so that she can run very fast.

4 Add her face and color her yellow with lots of dark spots.

How about a meerkat?

1 First draw an oblong shape for his body.

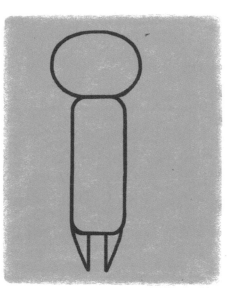

2 Add his round head and small legs.

3 He has round ears, small arms and little feet.

4 Give him a face and a tail, and color him in.

Can you draw a shark?

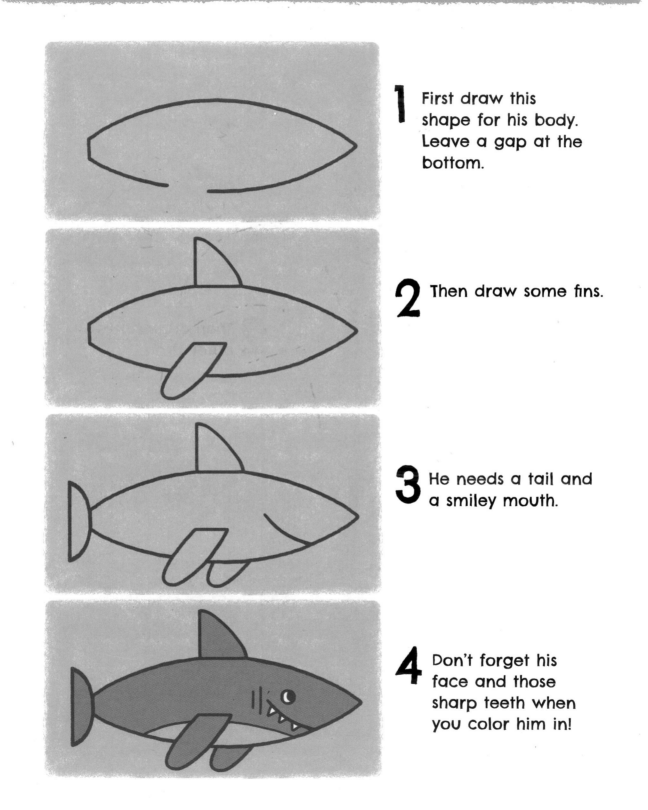

1 First draw this shape for his body. Leave a gap at the bottom.

2 Then draw some fins.

3 He needs a tail and a smiley mouth.

4 Don't forget his face and those sharp teeth when you color him in!

Let's try an octopus.

1 Start with his head.

2 Then draw his two outer arms.

3 He needs six more arms!

4 Give him a happy face and color in all those arms!

Try drawing a dolphin.

1 Start with this shape for his body. Leave a gap at the bottom.

2 Add some fins to help him swim.

3 Draw his tail and a long nose.

4 Add his smiley face and color him in. Now he's ready for a swim!

Draw a great big whale!

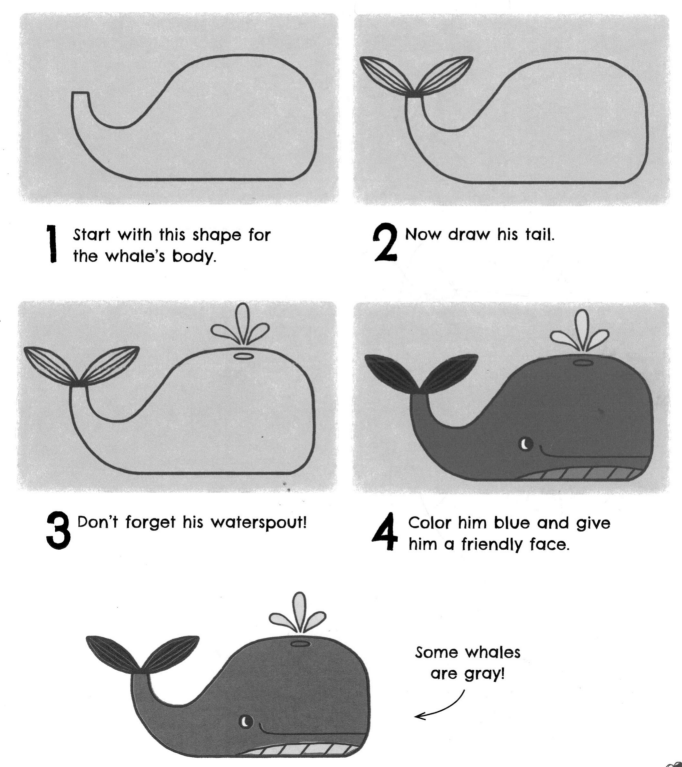

1 Start with this shape for the whale's body.

2 Now draw his tail.

3 Don't forget his waterspout!

4 Color him blue and give him a friendly face.

Some whales are gray!

Learn to draw a starfish.

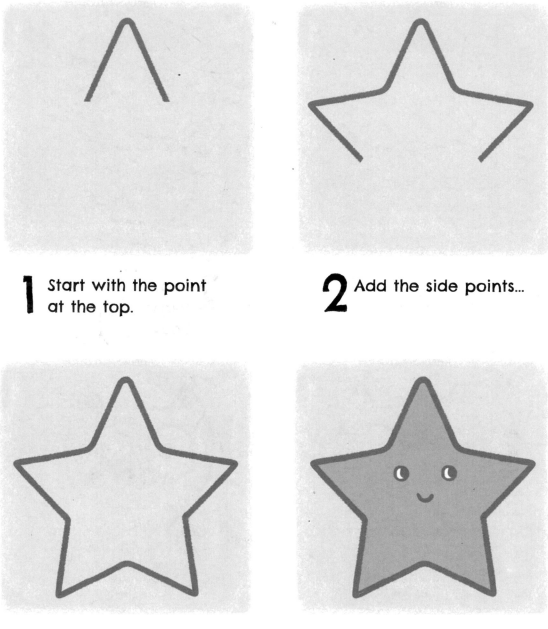

1 Start with the point at the top.

2 Add the side points...

3 ...and points at the bottom.

4 Give him a happy face and make him the color of sand.

Try a wise old owl.

1 She has a large head and little ears.

2 Add this smaller shape for her body.

3 She needs big round eyes, a beak and little feet. She's almost finished!

4 Draw some feathers on her chest, two wings and color her in.

Draw a caterpillar.

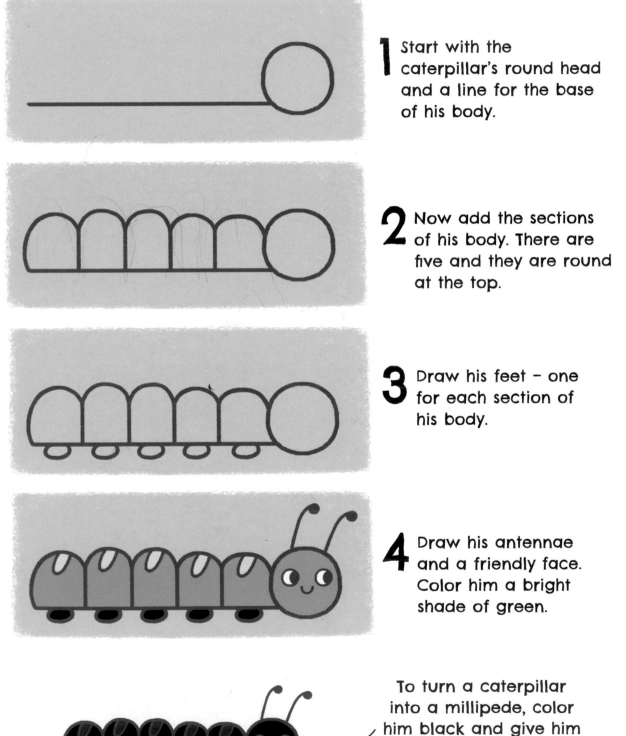

1 Start with the caterpillar's round head and a line for the base of his body.

2 Now add the sections of his body. There are five and they are round at the top.

3 Draw his feet – one for each section of his body.

4 Draw his antennae and a friendly face. Color him a bright shade of green.

To turn a caterpillar into a millipede, color him black and give him lots of little legs!

Now try a butterfly.

1 Start with a long oval shape for her body.

2 Now add the top sections of her wings.

3 Add the bottom sections of her wings and draw some stripes across her body.

4 Give her two antennae and a happy face. Decorate and color in her wings.

Try lots of different patterns and shades!

Let's draw a buzzy bee.

1 First draw the bee's round head.

2 Then add his body.

3 Don't forget the stripes on his body and two wings at the top.

4 Draw his antennae, face and six legs. Color him brightly!

Now try a ladybug.

1 Start by drawing a semicircle for her head and a straight line for the center of her body.

2 Now add a round shape to complete her body.

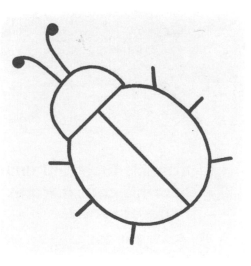

3 Draw her antennae and six little legs – three on each side.

4 Give her a cute face and lots of spots. Color her bright red and black.

How about a reindeer?

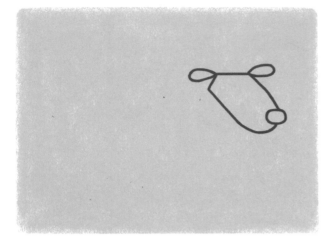

1 Start with his head. He has small ears and a round nose.

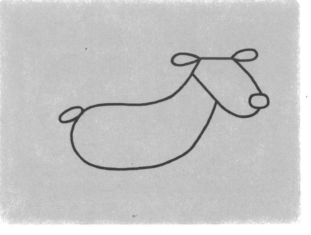

2 Now draw this shape for his body and a little tail.

3 Draw his legs as if he is running through the snow!

4 Draw his face and antlers. Color his coat a warm shade of brown.

Add a saddle, collar and red nose … and you have Rudolph!

Let's try a Pterodactyl.

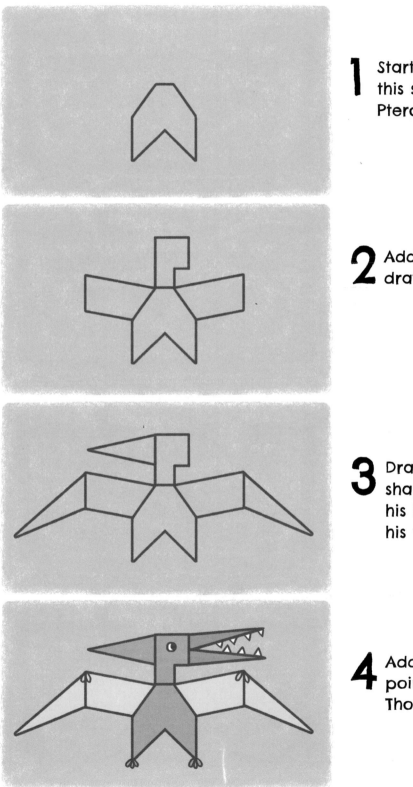

1 Start by drawing this shape for the Pterodactyl's body.

2 Add his head and start drawing his wings.

3 Draw a triangular shape on the back of his head. Then complete his wings.

4 Add claws, an eye and pointed jaws to finish. Those teeth look sharp!

Draw a Triceratops.

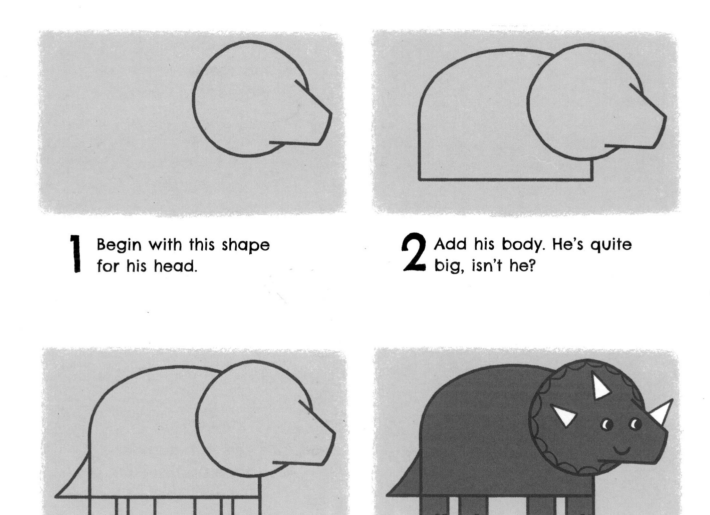

1 Begin with this shape for his head.

2 Add his body. He's quite big, isn't he?

3 Draw his tail and his little stumpy legs.

4 Add his face and color him in – don't forget he has three horns!

Then try a Diplodocus.

1 First draw this shape for his body.

2 Then add four strong legs.

3 He has a little head, a long neck and huge tail.

4 Draw his face and color him in. This Diplodocus has purple spots!

Glossary

antennae Two long, thin body parts on the head of insects and other animals, used to feel and smell.

antlers Two bony growths on the head of a deer.

Diplodocus A huge dinosaur that used to eat plants.

fin A flat part of the body of a fish used for balance and swimming.

mane The long hair on the neck and back of an animal.

millipede A small wormlike animal with many legs that is hard on the outside.

oblong A shape that is longer than it is wide.

Pterodactyl A flying reptile that lived at the same time as the dinosaurs.

Triceratops A dinosaur with three horns that ate plants.

trunk The long snout of an elephant used to breathe, feed and pick up things.

Further reading

Drawing Animals from A to Z (Walter Foster Jr, 2015)

How to Draw Dinosaurs by Fiona Watt (Usborne Publishing Ltd, 2013)

It's Fun to Draw Sea Creatures by Mark Bergin (Sky Pony Press, 2013)

Junior How to Draw Wild Animals by Kate Thompson (Top That Publishing, 2011)

Learn to Draw Rainforest & Jungle Animals by Robbin Cuddy (Walter Foster Jr, 2013)

Step-by-Step Drawing Animals by Fiona Watt (Usborne Publishing Ltd, 2015)

Websites

For web resources related to the subject of this book, go to: **www.windmillbooks.com/weblinks** and select this book's title.

Index

B
bee 24
big cats
    cheetah 14
    leopard 11
    lion 10
    lioness 11
    tiger 11
butterfly 23

C
caterpillar 22
cats *see* big cats
cheetah 14
crocodile 6

D
dinosaurs
    Diplodocus 29
    Pterodactyl 27
    Triceratops 28
Diplodocus 29
dolphin 18

E
elephant 8

G
gazelle 12
giraffe 9
gorilla 7

H
hippo 13

I
insects
    bee 24
    butterfly 23
    caterpillar 22
    ladybird 25
    millipede 22

L
ladybug 25
leopard 11
lion 10
lioness 11

M
meerkat 15
millipede 22

O
octopus 17
owl 21

P
Pterodactyl 27

R
reindeer 26
rhinoceros 5

S
sea creatures
    dolphin 18
    octopus 17
    shark 16
    starfish 20
    whale 19
shark 16
starfish 20

T
tiger 11
Triceratops 28

W
whale 19

Z
zebra 4